Yo-Yo Tricks

Amazing Yo-Yo Tricks for Kids!

By S. Daly

D1509617

THE SLEEPER

The Sleeper is a really easy trick, where your yo-yo spins freely at the bottom of the string. It is the best way to get better with your yo-yo technique. For trick execution is most important thing when you throw, and you have to throw it perfect - not too hard (if so, the yo-yo will bounce back up). You can be precise, so the throw isn't too hard, whit supporting the yo-yo with your hand.

Step by step
1. Throw the yo-yo with a lot of power
2. Keep spinning the yo-yo
3. Support the yo-yo with your hand
4. Watch out that the yo-yo doesn't bounce back up

THE SLEEPER

WALKING THE DOG

Walking the dog is the easiest trick for every yo-yo player. The technique of throwing is pretty much the same as the Sleeper. So, when the yo-yo is freely spinning you should put it down on the floor, so it can move around. Now it looks like you are walking the dog.
There are two important things to keep in mind when performing this trick. You have to keep your string tight all the time and you could make this trick better if you fling a Sleeper behind you before touching the floor, so it can gain more momentum.

Step by step
1. Throw the yo-yo
2. Keep spinning the yo-yo
3. Keep the string tight
4. Slowly put the yo-yo down on the floor
5. Let the yo-yo move around

**WALKING
THE DOG**

THE CREEPER

The Creeper is similar to Walking the dog. You start with a Sleeper again, but this time you get on your knees and tug the yo-yo back to you.

Step by step
1. Throw the yo-yo
2. Keep spinning the yo-yo
3. Get on your knees
4. Tug the yo-yo back to you

THE CREEPER

AROUND THE WORLD

Around the world is another easy, pretty basic trick in yo-yoing Begin with Sleeper, but now band your arm and throw your yo-yo over your elbow and let the string rest on your arm. You must leave the yo-yo spinning like that for some time and then, with just a little push you return it to your hand.

Step by step
1. Throw the yo-yo
2. Keep spinning the yo-yo
3. Bend your arm
4. Throw the yo-yo over your elbow
5. Push the yo-yo to return back to your hand

AROUND THE WORLD

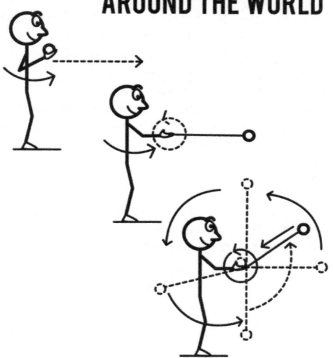

RIDING THE ELEVATOR

Riding the elevator is a bit complicated the first few times. Start with a normal throw of your yo-yo, next put a finger on your other hand under the string to pull the yo-yo back to you. When the yo-yo is back up again you land the gap of the yo-yo in the string held in your dominant hand and pull both carefully apart. Now you will get the impression that the yo-yo is climbing up, the impression of an elevator.

Step by step
1. Throw the yo-yo
2. Put a finger from the free hand under the string
3. Pull the yo-yo back up
4. With the dominant hand land the gap of the yo-yo on the string
5. Pull both hands carefully apart

RIDING THE ELEVATOR

THE FLYING TRAPEZE

The flying trapeze is a lot alike Riding the elevator. Again you start with normal throw down, then wrap the string around a finger on the other hand and let it land on its string. Next you bring your hands slowly together at the top and allow the yo-yo to roll back and forth.

Step by step
1. Throw the yo-yo
2. Wrap a string around a finger on your free hand
3. Land it on its string
4. Bring the hands slowly together at the top
5. Roll the yo-yo back and forth

THE FLYING TRAPEZE

ROCK THE BABY

At the beginning you let the yo-yo hang. Then you need to (with your free hand) pinch the string and pull it up and again you pinch both strings together at the bottom. Now flip the yo-yo and spread your fingers on your free hand to create a triangular shape.

Step by step
1. Throw the yo-yo
2. Let the yo-yo hang
3. With the free hand pinch the string
4. Pull the string up
5. With the free hand pinch both strings at the bottom
6. Flip the yo-yo
7. Spread the fingers on the free hand

ROCK
THE BABY

THROW THE BABY

Throw the baby is an update of Rock the baby, so you have to be good in performing it to go to this one. While you are making Rock the baby you have to move your fingers to pinch the string together away to the side and spin your yo-yo repeatedly towards yourself while throwing it in the air.

Step by step
1. Make "Rock the baby"
2. Move the fingers so you pinch the string together away
3. Throw yo-yo in the air
4. While throwing yo-yo in the air, spin it repeatedly towards yourself

THROW THE BABY

ONE HANDED STAR

To perform this trick you can use only your dominant hand. When performing it you bring your thumb up under the string and lift it. Now you wrap the string around your ring finger, next around your little finger, then middle finger and for the end your are around your thumb. Now slowly spread all your fingers apart so you get the shape of a star.

Step by step
1. Throw the yo-yo
2. Let the yo-yo hang
3. Bring the thumb on the dominant hand under the string
4. Lift the string
5. Wrap the string around the little finger, middle finger and the thumb
6. Slowly spread the fingers apart

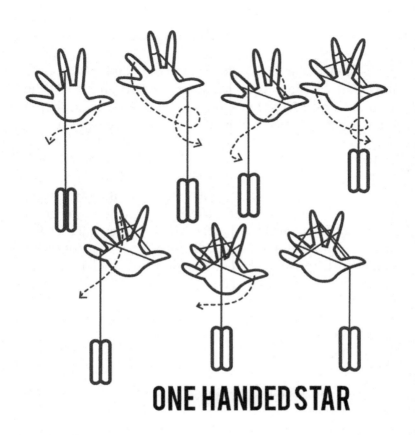

ONE HANDED STAR

TWO HANDED STAR

Two handed star is similar to the One handed star, only now you use both your hands for performing it. At the beginning you let the yo-yo hang, then you take a thumb on your free hand to pull the string across and a ring finger on the dominant hand to pull it back so the V shape is formed. Next you lift up the remaining string, with your pointer finger on the free hand, so it is hanging over the finger and all together hanging over the star. Then you pull the remaining string, with a thumb on a dominant hand, in the biggest whole in the star. At the end you pull with your middle finger on the dominant hand down in front of your star and use it to lift up the string that remained. Again, all of this should form a shape of a star.

Step by step
1. Throw the yo-yo
2. Let the yo-yo hang
3. With a thumb on the free hand pull the string across
4. With a ring finger on the dominant hand pull the string back
5. With a pointer finger on the free hand lift up the remaining string
6. With a thumb on the dominant hand pull the string up in the biggest whole in the star
7. Pull down a middle finger on the dominant hand in front of your star and lift up the string that remained

TWO HANDED STAR

THE EIFFEL TOWER

For start you let your yo-yo hang. Next you lift the string with the back of the free hand, leaving free only your thumb as you will need it for the rest of the trick. Next you lift the string again with the back of the thumb on the dominant hand so an open rectangular is shaped. Now you have to twist your free had and make a figure of eight from the strings. Take a pointer finger on you free hand, pick up the remaining strings and pull everything up through this figure of eight, supporting the string only with your pointer finger. At the end just grab the remaining strings to complete the formation, using just your ring and middle fingers on the dominant hand.

Step by step
1. Throw the yo-yo
2. Let the yo-yo hang
3. Lift the string with the back of the free hand
4. Leave a thumb on the free hand free for continue the trick
5. With the back of a thumb on the dominant hand lift the string up, again
6. Twist the free hand
7. With a pointer finger on the free hand pick up the remaining strings
8. Pull everything up through the figure
9. Let the string be supported only by the pointer finger on the free hand
10. With the ring finger and middle finger on the dominant hand simply grab the remaining strings

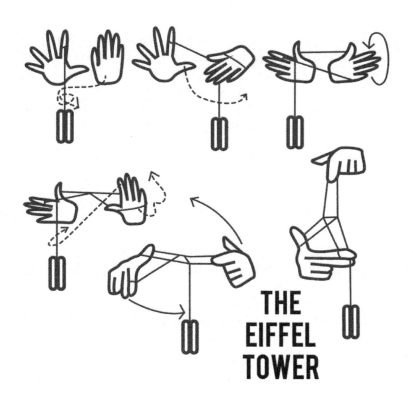

**THE
EIFFEL
TOWER**

THE CROSS

The cross is much alike The Eiffel tower. For start you leave your yo-yo hanging, then you lift the string up with your free hand. Once again lift the string, only now with the thumb on your dominant hand. Now you twist your free hand and form a shape of eight. Let the string hang from both of your thumbs and the pointer finger on tour free hand. At the end just pinch the strings together to make a cross.

Step by step
1. Throw the yo-yo
2. Let the yo-yo hang
3. With the free hand lift the string up
4. With the thumb on the dominant hand lift the string up again
5. Twist the free hand
6. Let the string hang from both of the thumbs and a pointer finger on the free hand
7. Pinch the string together

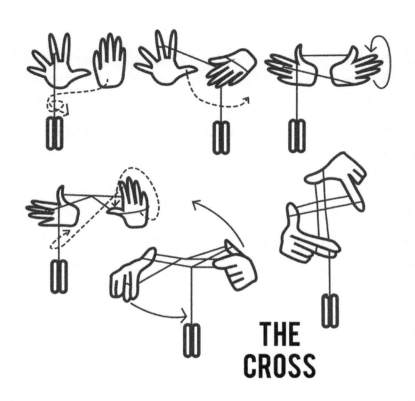

THE CROSS

THE DOG BITE

The dog bit is an easier trick. The most important thing in the trick are your clothing and your yo-yo, of course. To make the trick work it is best to wear a loose pants and have a thin and responsive yo-yo.

First you throw your yo-yo forwards, then backwards between your legs and for the end you snap it forwards towards your leg. If you did everything correct the yo-yo should now grab your pants and stay there.

Step by step
   1. Throw the yo-yo forwards
   2. Swing the yo-yo backwards
   3. Snap the yo-yo forwards towards the leg

THE DOG BITE

THE RATTLESNAKE

First you throw a Sleeper, except now you throw it on a side. Next you bring you bring your free leg against the strings so it will make a rattling sound. Now the whole thing looks like a rattlesnake.

Step by step
1. Throw the yo-yo
2. Keep the yo-yo spinning
3. Bring the free leg against the string

THE RATTLESNAKE

SHOOTING THE MOON

For start just throw your yo-yo and circle with it in a semi circles above your head. When it lose its speed just snap it in front of you, wait till it returns and flick it up to repeat the whole trick.

Step by step
1. Throw the yo-yo
2. Swing with the yo-yo in a semi circles above the head
3. When it lose its speed snap the yo-yo in front of you
4. Flick it up again

SHOOTING THE MOON

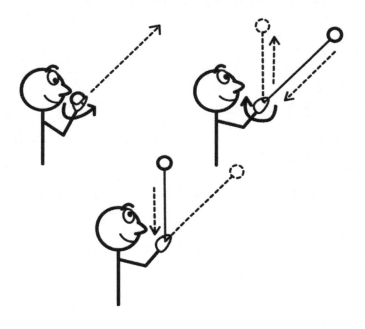

THE TUNNEL

Beginning is like in the Around the world, when the yo-yo in front of you, you should quickly spread your legs and let it swing through them and let it roll back up in your hand.

Step by step
1. Throw the yo-yo
2. Keep spinning the yo-yo
3. Quickly spread the legs, when the yo-yo falls in front of you
4. Let the yo-yo swing through the legs
5. Allow the yo-yo roll back up in the hand

THE TUNNEL

THE ELEPHANT

First you have to set up a light chair near to you. The you start with a Sleeper, which is thrown in the direction of the chair. While doing this let the yo-yo swing over the chair and spin. The whole thing together looks an elephant's trunk.

Step by step
1. Set a chair near to you
2. Throw the yo-yo in the direction of the chair
3. Allow the yo-yo to swing over the chair while spinning

THE ELEPHANT

FINGER SPINNING

This is one of the most unique tricks. It is better for you, when performing this trick, if you have a wider yo-yo which can rest the side of it easily on your fingers without falling. It is known that the best yo-yos for this trick are made of metal and they are curved, so your fingers can hold them.

First you have to throw the yo-yo in the opposite direction of your body. Next you catch it with your free hand and use your dominant hand to maintain the tension in the string. This way is much easier to learn then to do everything with your free hand.

Step by step
1. Throw the yo-yo at a slight angle in the opposite direction off your body
2. Catch the cupped side with the finger
3. Gently bring finger down and maintain control over the spin

FINGER SPINNING

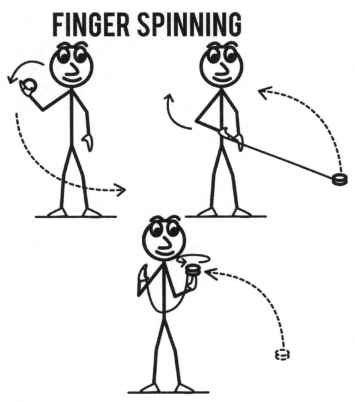

SLACK TRAPEZE

Other name for this trick is Slack whip. First you start, with your free hand, pinching and swinging the string upwards, while keeping it slack. Now you swing the string over your free hand's wrist, snap it and pull it tightly. Next you swing the yo-yo over your free hand and around your dominant hand into a trapeze.

Step by step
1. Throw the yo-yo
2. With the free hand pinch and swing the string upwards
3. Swing the string over the wrist on the hand
4. Snap the string and pull it tightly
5. Swing the yo-yo over the free hand and around the dominant hand

SLACK TRAPEZE

REVERSE SLACK TRAPEZE

Begin with throwing normal Slack trapeze. Then with your free hand pinch the string. Next you have to use your dominant hand to quickly snap the string down and at the same time you have to bring the remaining string under and around your wrist on a free hand. At the end just pull the string tight and swing the yo-yo.

Step by step
1. Make normal trapeze
2. Pinch the string with the free hand
3. With the dominant hand quickly snap the string down
4. At the same time bring the remaining string under and around the wrist on the free hand
5. Pull the string tight
6. Swing the yo-yo

REVERSE SLACK TRAPEZE

DOUBLE TRAPEZE

Once again you begin with a normal Slack trapeze, just this time you wrap the yo-yo twice around the dominant hand. At the end you just have to snap the yo-yo out of a trapeze and that's it.

Step by step
1. Make a normal trapeze
2. Wrap the yo-yo twice around the dominant hand
3. Snap the yo-yo out of the trapeze

DOUBLE
TRAPEZE

THE TSUNAMI

For start throw the Sleeper. Then you bring the string over the index finger on the dominant hand and swing the yo-yo again to bring the string over the index finger on the free hand now. At the end you have to swing the yo-yo once again over the index finger on the free hand.

Step by step
1. Throw the yo-yo
2. Keep the yo-yo spinning
3. Bring the string over the index finger on the dominant hand
4. Swing the yo-yo to repeat the same action over the index finger on the free hand
5. Swing the yo-yo again over the index finger on the free hand

TSUNAMI

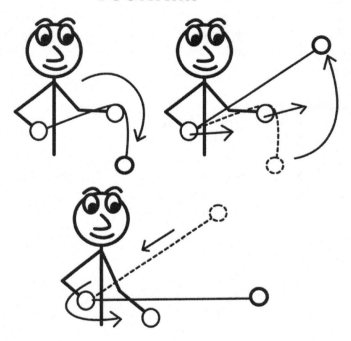

ELI HOP

Begin with a Slack trapeze. Now throw your yo-yo up and bring your hands quickly together. While yo-yo is falling back down bring the dominant hand away from your free hand and catch the yo-yo on the string, so it lands in a trapeze.

Step by step
1. Make a normal trapeze
2. Throw the yo-yo up
3. Bring both hands close together
4. As the yo-yo is falling down bring the dominant hand away from the free hand
5. Catch the yo-yo on the string

ELI HOP

THE PLASTIC WHIP

For start you should to throw the Sleeper. Now you have to hold your hand with a palm facing to your left and aloe the string to hand over your thumb. Next you snap it forward, so it creates a loop of string that can fall into a gap, causing the yo-yo hang.

Step by step
1. Throw the yo-yo
2. Keep the yo-yo spinning
3. Hold the hand with a palm facing to your left (if you are a right handed)
4. Let the string hang over your thumb
5. Snap the yo-yo forward

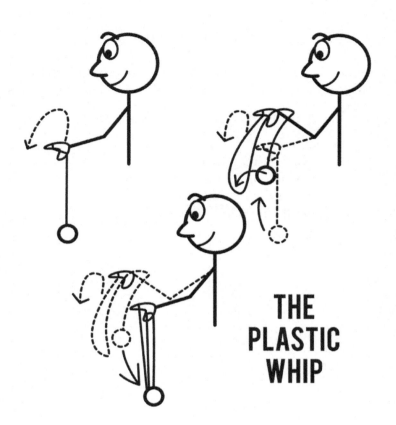

THE PLASTIC WHIP

THE IRON WHIP

Begin with a Slack trapeze. Now create a loop, snap your yo-yo up and whip the loop back down to return to a trapeze.

Step by step
1. Make a normal trapeze
2. Create a loop
3. Snap your yo-yo up
4. Whip the loop back down

THE
IRON WHIP

UNDERMOUNT

Begin with a Sleeper, just now throw it away from your body and the index finger on your free hand under the string. Then you use the dominant hand to pull down while raising the yo-yo so it swings towards you. At the end you swing the yo-yo into the string and bring your hand back around the yo-yo.

Step by step
1. Throw the yo-yo away from the body
2. Keep the yo-yo spinning
3. Put the index finger on the free hand under the string
4. Pull down the dominant hand while raising the yo-yo
5. Swing the yo-yo
6. Bring the hand up around the yo-yo

UNDERMOUNT

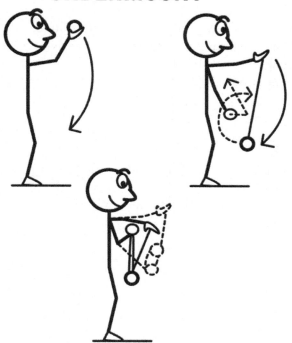

OVERMOUNT

Like in the Undermount you begin again with the Sleeper. Only now you pull your index finger on the free hand back against the string, so the whole yo-yo is positioned against the string. Now loose the hold with the dominant hand so the yo-yo can swing in a loop.

Step by step
1. Throw the yo-yo away from the body
2. Keep the yo-yo spinning
3. Pull the index finger on the free hand back against the string
4. Loose the hold with the dominant hand

OVERMOUNT

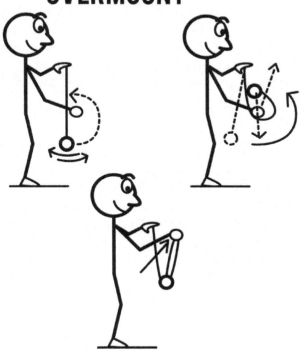

OVER AND UNDER

Begin with the Undermount, but now swing the yo-yo back out of it. Next you let the yo-yo swing up and around your ring (or middle) finger and into an Overmount. At the end you pop the yo-yo again out of the Overmount and back into the Undermount. You can do this repeatedly.

Step by step
1. Throw the yo-yo away from your body
2. Keep the yo-yo spinning
3. Swing the yo-yo out of the Undermount
4. Let the yo-yo swing up and around the ring or middle finger and into Overmount
5. Pop the yo-yo out of the Overmount and back into Undermount

OVER AND UNDER

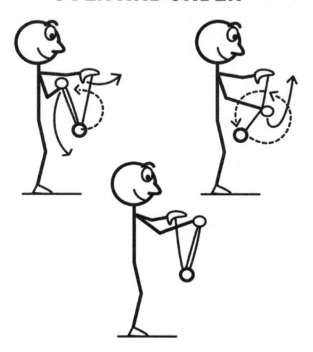

BRAINTWISTER

You begin with the Undermount, but now you put your dominant hand under the free hand. Then you pull the dominant hand back against the string and upwards, in order to sling the yo-yo. Once again you sling your yo-yo over the dominant hand and swing it down.

Step by step
1. Throw the yo-yo away from the body
2. Keep the yo-yo spinning
3. Put the dominant hand back against the string and upwards
4. Sling the yo-yo
5. Again sling the yo-yo over the dominant hand
6. Swing the yo-yo down

BRAIN TWISTER

SPLIT BOTTOM MOUNT

Start with the Sleeper. While pulling the dominant hand down you have to put your index finger on the free hand under the string. Now press the index finger on the other hand in the string and flip the yo-yo around. For the end you have to pull the free hand down and form a loop.

Step by step
1. Throw the yo-yo
2. Keep the yo-yo spinning
3. Pull the dominant hand down
4. Put the index finger on the free hand under the string
5. Press the other index finger into the string
6. Flip the yo-yo around
7. Pull the free hand down

SPLIT BOTTOM MOUNT

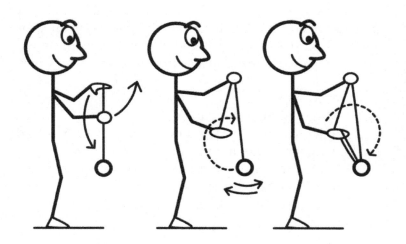

BARREL ROLL

Start with a Split bottom mount. Now pull your free hand under the yo-yo and your dominant hand over the yo-yo. Next bring the yo-yo over the index finger on your dominant hand into the strings and repeat that with your free hand, so the yo-yo will land in a split bottom mount at the end. You can make this as many times as you want.

Step by step
1. Make "Split bottom mount"
2. Pull the free hand down under and put the dominant hand up over the yo-yo
3. Bring the yo-yo over the index finger on the dominant hand into the string
4. Repeat last step with the free hand

BARREL ROLL

SMASHING THE ATOM

Begin with a Split bottom mount. Then, with your free hand, pass the yo-yo forward, after that, with your dominant hand, pass it backwards and perform three somersaults. Now you let drop the string on the index finger of the dominant hand to fall into the Undermount.

Step by step
1. Make "Split bottom mount"
2. With the free hand pass the yo-yo forward
3. With the dominant hand pass the yo-yo backwards
4. Perform three somersaults
5. Drop the string on the index finger on the dominant hand to fall into an Undermount

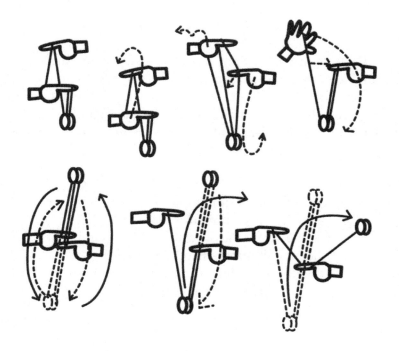

SMASHING THE ATOM

BOING BOING

Again begin with a Split bottom mount. When the yo-yo lands you have to snap it forwards and let it continue to move forwards. Now you slide the dominant hand downwards to accommodate this and the quickly snap it back up. With your hand slipping back down again you can do this continuously.

Step by step
1. Make "Split bottom mount"
2. Snap the yo-yo forwards
3. Let the yo-yo move forwards
4. Slide the dominant hand downwards
5. Quickly snap the dominant hand back up
6. Let the hand slip back down again

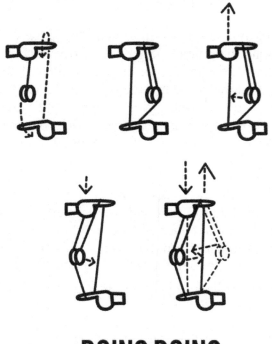

BOING BOING

DOUBLE OR NOTHING

For start throw the yo-yo across your body. Now loop the string around the pointer finger on the free hand and over and around your index finger on the dominant hand. You should keep some space between, though. Then you have to continue to loop the string up over your free hand again and land the yo-yo on the string between both fingers. As a result you should get a small trapeze.

Step by step
1. Throw the yo-yo across the body
2. Loop the string around the pointer finger on the free hand and over and around the index finger on the dominant hand, but keep some space between
3. Continue to loop the string up over the free hand
4. Land the yo-yo on the string between both fingers

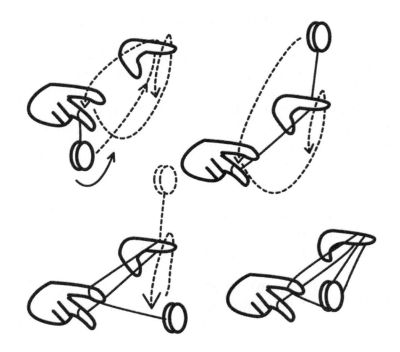

DOUBLE OR NOTHING

POP AND FRESH

Start with the Split bottom mount. Now you snap the yo-yo up in the air. While the yo-yo is up you have to switch your hands, passing your free hand over the yo-yo. This should end in a mount. Now you snap the yo-yo once more and switch your hands back in the starting position. The end of the trick is landing you the yo-yo in the Split bottom mount again.

Step by step
1. Make "Split bottom mount"
2. Snap the yo-yo up in the air
3. Switch the hands, passing the free hand over the yo-yo
4. Snap the yo-yo in the air again
5. Switch the hands back

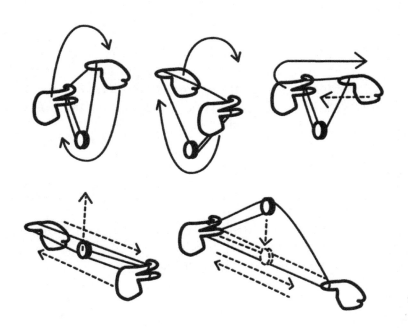

POP AND FRESH

MACH 5

Begin with a Split bottom mount. Put the free hand under the yo-yo towards yourself. Now you pull it up first, then away and down to hang the yo-yo between your hands. Now you have to rotate your hands around the yo-yo. You can make this repeatedly.

Step by step
1. Make "Split bottom mount"
2. Put the free hand under the yo-yo towards yourself
3. Pull the yo-yo up, then away and down to hang yo-yo between the hands
4. Rotate the hands around the yo-yo

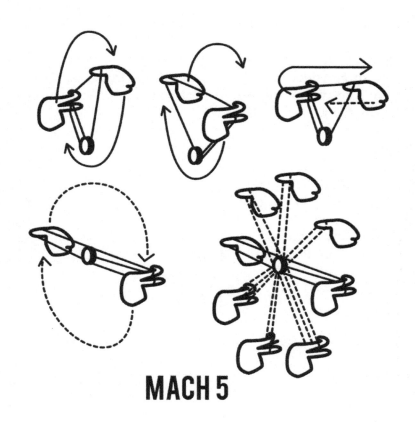

MACH 5

HIDEMASA HOOK

For start leave the yo-yo hang. Now pull it up and snap the string under your index finger of the free hand. Once you catch the string back in the gap you have to pull it really tight.

Step by step
1. Let the yo-yo hang
2. Pull the yo-yo up
3. Snap the string under the index finger on the free hand
4. Catch the string in the gap
5. Pull the string really tight

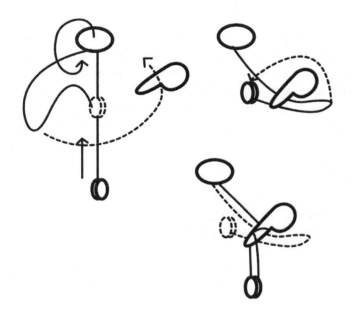

HIDEMASA HOOK

COLD FUSION

Begin with performing Double or nothing. Now bring both hands under the yo-yo and catch it on the string. Next push the strings to catch the yo-yo again on the first string and again on the second string. After that, remove your finger. The result should be landing it on a one and a half mount. At the end you pass the yo-yo over the free hand and twist it trice on mount. You can make this repeatedly.

Step by step
1. Make "Double or nothing"
2. Bring the hands under the yo-yo to catch it on the string
3. Push the strings to catch the yo-yo again on the first string and then on the outside string
4. Remove the finger
5. Pass the yo-yo over the free hand and twist it trice on the mount

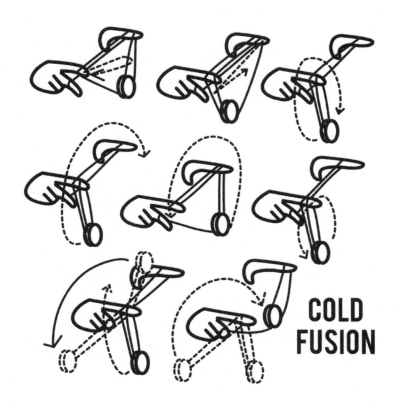

COLD
FUSION

Fun facts about yo-yo

- Yo-yos are essentially toys, generally composed of two cylindrical discs connected by an axle, with an attached string.

- Terracotta examples of yo-yos have been found in Ancient Greek art dating between 400 – 500 BC.

- The first modern patent of a yo-yo was in 1866 by James Haven and Charles Hettrich, and it was named a 'whirligig' and a 'bandalore'.

- International yo-yo competitions, where performance is judged, are held all over the world every year, with contestants from many backgrounds.

- The term 'yo-yo' possibly came from one of the languages spoken in the Philippines, from a word meaning 'come back' or 'spring', although its origins are uncertain.

- A yo-yo has also been called a 'bandalore' (a French term) and a 'quiz', and was named a 'yo-yo' in 1928 in the United States, by Pedro Flores, who was a Filipino immigrant.

- One of the most common yo-yo tricks is 'walk the dog', which is when the toy appears to be spinning along the ground in front of your feet.

- Cheap yo-yos can spin approximately 10-20 seconds, with a record of nearly 4 minutes, while professional ball bearing yo-yos can spin for 1-4 minutes, with a record of just over 21 minutes.

- Yo-yos are generally symmetrical, with weight distributed more on the edges of the discs, although this can vary.

- Yo-yos are now one of the hottest toy collectibles and many models have values in the 100's even thousands of dollars.

- Originally manufacturing yo-yos from wood, yo-yo technology improved in the 1960s when the industry switched to plastic. Benefits of a plastic yo-yo include the uniform weight distribution only possible with plastic, as the natural variations in wood density are undesirable for an even spin.

- The first metal yoyos were created and in the 1990's the yo-yo world championships started.

- Most modern yo-yos are made from a "take-apart" design, designed to be taken easily apart and reassembled by the player. This design was first created by Tom Kuhn. This enables the replacement of yo-yo components, including the string, renewable friction sources, or even trans-axle components.

Made in the USA
Monee, IL
01 November 2021